How a Bill Becomes a Law

Kyla Steinkraus

rourkeeducationalmedia.com

*Scan for Related Titles
and Teacher Resources*

Before Reading:

Building Academic Vocabulary and Background Knowledge

Before reading a book, it is important to tap into what your child or students already know about the topic. This will help them develop their vocabulary, increase their reading comprehension, and make connections across the curriculum.

1. Look at the cover of the book. What will this book be about?
2. What do you already know about the topic?
3. Let's study the Table of Contents. What will you learn about in the book's chapters?
4. What would you like to learn about this topic? Do you think you might learn about it from this book? Why or why not?
5. Use a reading journal to write about your knowledge of this topic. Record what you already know about the topic and what you hope to learn about the topic.
6. Read the book.
7. In your reading journal, record what you learned about the topic and your response to the book.
8. After reading the book complete the activities below.

Content Area Vocabulary
Read the list. What do these words mean?

amended
approval
bill
Congress
debate
filibustering
law
majority
pass
representative
sponsors
veto

After Reading:

Comprehension and Extension Activity

After reading the book, work on the following questions with your child or students in order to check their level of reading comprehension and content mastery.

1. Explain why a bill might go from the House of Representatives to Congress and then back to the House of Representatives. (Summarize)
2. What government branches process and create laws? (Asking questions)
3. What is the majority for the House of Representatives? For the Senate? (Summarize)
4. What happens if the bill is not made into a law? (Asking questions)
5. Explain the checks and balances process. (Summarize)

Extension Activity

You are a normal citizen that has an idea for a new law. Write a letter to your state representative describing your new law and why it is important. Be sure to address and sign your letter. You can find your state representative on your state's website.

Table of Contents

It ought to be a **law**! When new rules are needed for society, laws are put in place to protect people and guarantee their rights.

TRAFFIC LAWS STRICTLY ENFORCED

Laws also protect people from harm. For example, laws about following the speed limit and stopping at stop signs keep drivers safe.

HOUSE OF
REPRESENTATIVES

SENATE

The House and Senate work in the Capitol Building in Washington, D.C.

To make a new **law**, a certain process must be followed. To start with, every new law starts out as a bill. A bill outlines the details of a proposed law.

In the United States, the federal government makes and maintains laws. The legislative branch creates the laws. There are two chambers: the Senate and the House of Representatives. Together they are called **Congress**.

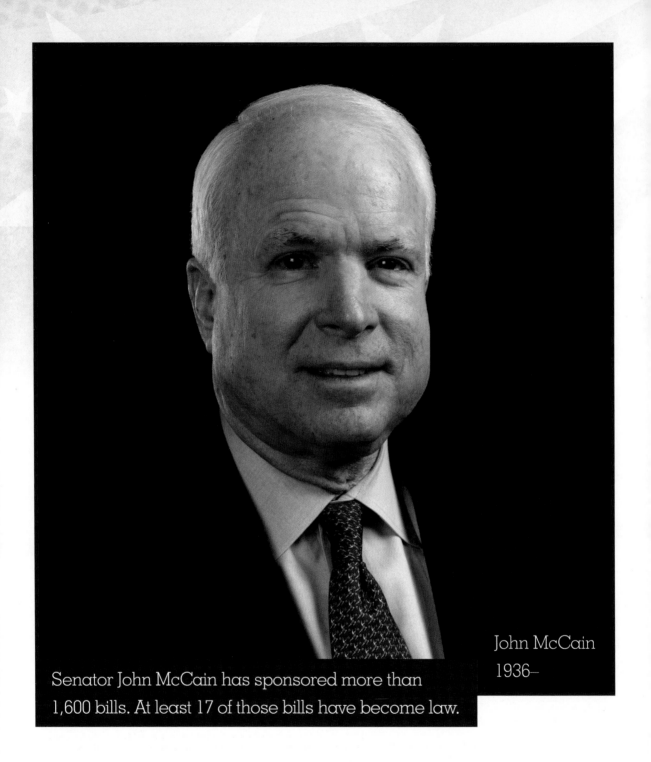

John McCain
1936–

Senator John McCain has sponsored more than 1,600 bills. At least 17 of those bills have become law.

When a member of Congress has an idea for a new law, he or she **sponsors** it. Some bills have many sponsors. The sponsor introduces the bill to the rest of Congress.

A citizen can suggest ideas for laws to their representatives. However, only a member of Congress can introduce the bill to be voted on in Congress.

Members of Congress talk with citizens of their state, to understand what issues are important and how they can help by passing new laws.

Once the bill is introduced, it must go through a process of **approval**. The Speaker of the House assigns the bill to a committee so it can be studied. The committee listens to experts to figure out what effects the bill could have if it became a law.

As Speaker of the House, John Boehner, decides which bills go to committee and when a bill will be presented to the House.

The committee can vote to **pass** the bill, revise it further, or put the bill aside, which is known as tabling. Only about 15 percent of bills are passed.

The members of the House Committee on Veterans Affairs consider testimony on a bill. Other committees that study important bills include the House Budget Committee, the Education and the Workforce Committee, and the Homeland Security Committee.

When a committee votes to pass a bill, they write a report describing the bill's purpose. They list all the reasons why the bill should be passed. The bill then goes on the calendar.

Writing a bill requires a lot of paper. Some bills are more than 1,000 pages!

Next, the House Rules Committee decides if the bill will be voted on quickly, debated, or **amended**.

When a bill is amended it is changed or additional terms are added to it. An addition to a bill is called an amendment.

The House Rules Committee helps the Speaker keep order.

On the Floor

Next, the bill goes to the floor of the House of Representatives. The members **debate** the bill and vote on it. If a **majority** of members vote yes, then the bill moves on to the Senate.

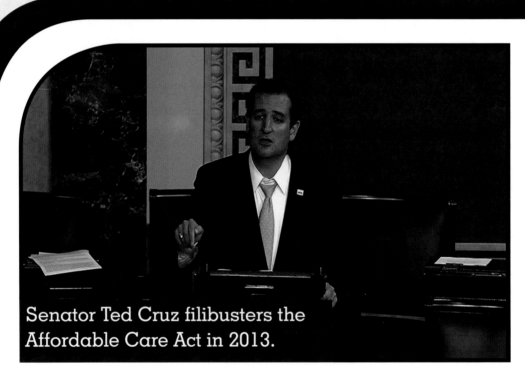

Senator Ted Cruz filibusters the Affordable Care Act in 2013.

The House has a time limit on debates, but the Senate does not. Sometimes a Congress member will try to prevent a bill from passing by **filibustering**. He or she delays the vote by giving a long speech. As long as the Congressperson keeps talking, the vote cannot take place.

When Congress votes on a bill, they may do it one of three ways.
1. A voice vote: Members state their vote as yea or nay.
2. A standing vote: If the majority of people stand, the vote passes.
3. Electronic vote: Representatives record their vote using the electronic voting system.

When the bill reaches the Senate, it is again assigned to a committee. The Senate studies the bill and either releases it, amends it, or tables it. If it is released, the bill is discussed and debated on the Senate floor.

A majority of 51 votes in the Senate will pass the bill. In the House, it takes 218 votes to pass a bill.

After the House and Senate both pass the bill, Congress still has one more job to do. When the Senate got the bill, they were allowed to make changes to it that the House did not vote on. For this reason, the bill goes to a conference committee.

Members of the House and Senate work out the differences between the two versions of the bill. Once they have a final version, it is sent back to both houses of Congress for final approval.

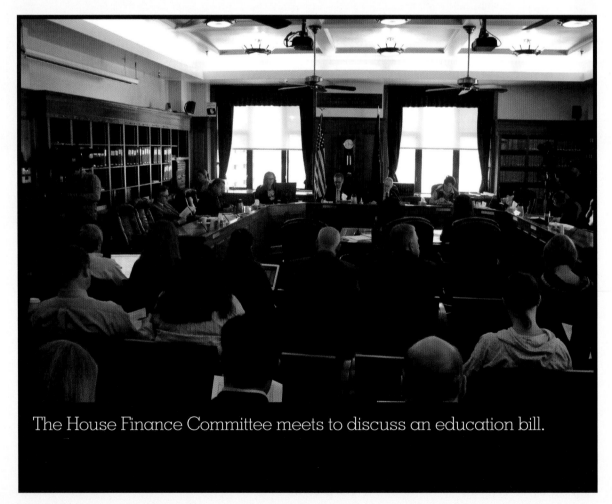

The House Finance Committee meets to discuss an education bill.

Finally, the bill is printed in a process called enrolling. The Speaker of the House and the vice president, who presides over the Senate, both sign the enrolled bill.

Representative John Boehner became the Speaker of the House in 2010.

The president's approval is the last step in the process. The president has ten days to sign the bill or to **veto**, or reject it.

When the president signs the bill, it officially becomes a law.

If the president doesn't sign or veto a bill within ten days, the bill still becomes a law.

President Franklin Delano Roosevelt signs the Social Security Bill in the White House. August 14, 1935

Sometimes there is a special signing ceremony when the president signs a bill into law. The president uses a different pen to sign each bill. If he is signing several bills that day, he will have several pens! After signing, he gives the pen to the bill's sponsors or to other people who care about the new law.

The president may offer the pen to a citizen who benefits from the new law, such as a law that improves education for students.

If the president vetoes the bill, there is still a chance that it can become a law. The vetoed bill goes back to Congress to be voted on again or changed to satisfy the president's objections.

After a veto, two-thirds of the Senate and two-thirds of the House must vote in favor of the bill for it to become a law without the president's signature.

Since 1789, presidents have vetoed 2,563 bills. Only 106 presidential vetoes have been overturned by Congress.

Even with so many people working on the laws, sometimes a law passes that is unfair. The Justices of the Supreme Court can overturn the law if it is unconstitutional, or contradicts the Constitution, our nation's most important set of laws.

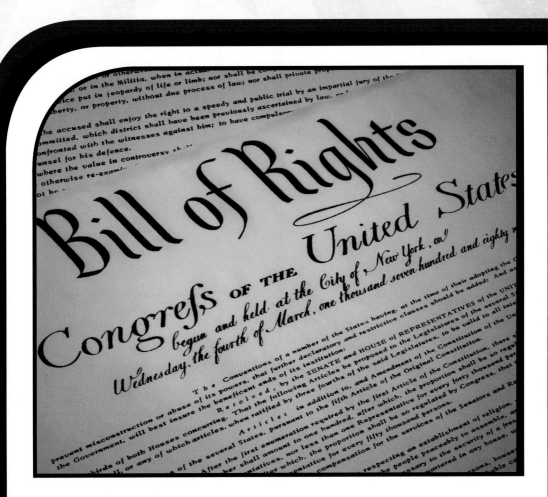

The Constitution was created over 200 years ago. It includes the Bill of Rights. The government cannot pass a law that would take away any of our rights, such as the right of freedom of speech, freedom of religion, or the right to vote.

There are many steps a bill must take in its journey to become a law. Laws are important to our society because they help keep us safe, maintain our rights, and help us settle differences peacefully.

Making a Law

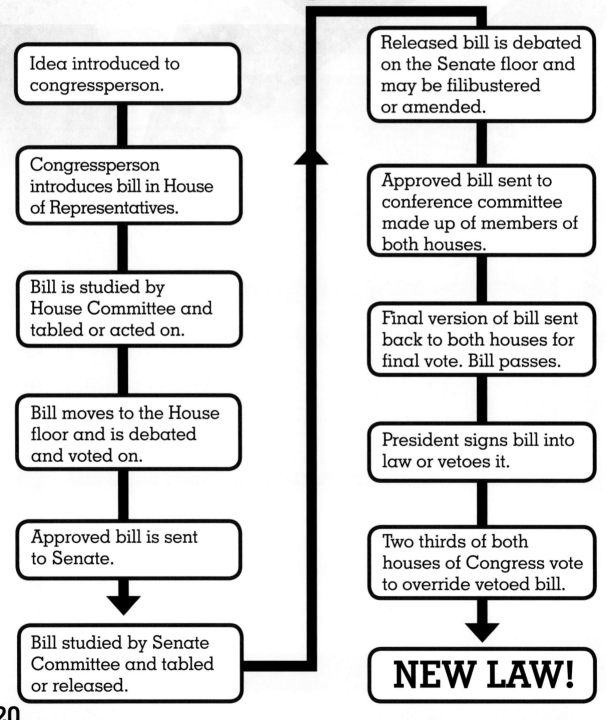

Idea introduced to congressperson.

Congressperson introduces bill in House of Representatives.

Bill is studied by House Committee and tabled or acted on.

Bill moves to the House floor and is debated and voted on.

Approved bill is sent to Senate.

Bill studied by Senate Committee and tabled or released.

Released bill is debated on the Senate floor and may be filibustered or amended.

Approved bill sent to conference committee made up of members of both houses.

Final version of bill sent back to both houses for final vote. Bill passes.

President signs bill into law or vetoes it.

Two thirds of both houses of Congress vote to override vetoed bill.

NEW LAW!

If you have an idea for a law, or if you have opinions about a bill that is already in Congress, you can call, email, or write letters to your **representative**. You can make a difference!

Glossary

amended (uh-MEND-id): improved or made better by making changes

approval (uh-PROOV-uhl): the act of officially accepting a plan

bill (bil): a written plan for a new law to be debated in Congress

Congress (KON-gres): the elected members of the House of Representatives and the Senate

debate (dih-BAYT): a formal discussion between people with different views

filibustering (fil-ih-BUHS-tir-een): a long speech given by a senator to try and defeat a bill

law (law): a rule made by the government that must be obeyed

majority (muh-JOR-ih-tee): more than half

pass (pas): to approve or make a new law

representative (reh-prih-ZEN-tuh-tiv): a person in the government chosen by the public through popular vote

sponsors (SPON-sorz): urges the passing of a bill

veto (VEE-toh): to reject a bill by not signing it

Index

Show What You Know

1. What is a bill?
2. Who can introduce a bill to Congress?
3. Why might a Congressperson filibuster a bill?
4. Explain how all states have an equal say in whether a law is passed.
5. Is it fair for the president to be allowed to veto a bill? Why or why not?

Websites to Visit

bensguide.gpo.gov/6-8/lawmaking
www.congressforkids.net/Legislativebranch_makinglaws.htm
kids.clerk.house.gov/grade-school/lesson.html?intID=17

About the Author

Kyla Steinkraus has written several letters to her representatives in Congress. They almost always write back. Kyla believes it is important to speak up and share our opinions with our government. We can always make a difference! She lives with her husband and two children in Tampa, Florida. She enjoys drawing, photography, and writing.

Meet The Author!
www.meetREMauthors.com

PHOTO CREDITS: title page © Africa Studio; page 4 © RobertH2255; page 5 © Martin Falbisoner; page 7 © AP Images/Scott Mcintyre; page 8, 9, 11, 15 © AP Images/J. Scott Applewhite; page 10 © Emir Memedovski; page 12 © AP Images; page 13 © Andriy Popov; page 14 © AP Images/Bohrer; page 16 © Library of Congress; page 17 © AP Images/Ron Sachs/picture-alliance/dpa; page 18 © Lawrence Jackson/White House; page 19 © leezsnow; page 21 © JenniferPhotographyImaging

Edited by: Jill Sherman

Cover by: Nicola Stratford, nicolastratford.com
Interior design by: Jen Thomas

Library of Congress PCN Data

How a Bill Becomes a Law / Kyla Steinkraus
 (U.S. Government and Civics)
  ISBN 978-1-62717-682-8 (hard cover)
  ISBN 978-1-62717-804-4 (soft cover)
  ISBN 978-1-62717-920-1 (e-Book)
Library of Congress Control Number: 2014935457

Printed in the United States of America, North Mankato, Minnesota

Also Available as:

ROURKE'S
e-Books